OUR
Martin Luther King
BOOK

by Patricia C. McKissack
illustrated by Helen Endres

ELGIN, ILLINOIS 60120

AUTHOR'S NOTE: The Martin Luther King, Jr. Center for Non-Violent Social Change has indicated that they would enjoy receiving cards from children. If you wish to make cards, as the children in this book did, mail them to the center at this address: 449 Auburn Street, NE, Atlanta, Georgia 30312.

PHOTO CREDITS: pp 5, 20—© Flip Schulke, Black Star; p 16—AP/Wide World Photos.

Distributed by Childrens Press, 1224 West Van Buren Street, Chicago, Illinois 60607.

Library of Congress Cataloging in Publication Data

McKissack, Pat, 1944-
    Our Martin Luther King book.

    (A Special-day book)
    Summary: Describes what a kindergarten class learned about Martin Luther King, Jr., on his birthday.
    1. King, Martin Luther—Juvenile literature.
2. Afro-Americans—Civil Rights—Juvenile literature.
3. Afro-Americans—Biography—Juvenile literature.
4. Baptists—United States—Clergy—Biography—Juvenile literature. [1. King, Martin Luther. 2. Civil rights workers. 3. Clergy. 4. Afro-Americans—Biography]
I. Endres, Helen, ill.   II. Title.   III. Series.
E185.97.K5M37 1986   323.4′092′4 [92]   86-6785
ISBN 0-89565-342-7

3 4 5 6 7 8 9 10 11 12 R 95 94 93 92 91 90 89 88 87

OUR
Martin Luther King
BOOK

This book is about how we celebrated Martin
Luther King, Jr.'s birthday in our class. You will
have more ideas in your class.

Mrs. Stevens showed us a January calendar. There was a circle around the third Monday.

"This is the day we will celebrate Dr. Martin Luther King, Jr.'s birthday. Do you know who Dr. King was?" she asked.

Not everyone knew.

"Martin Luther King, Jr. was a black, American, civil-rights leader," Mrs. Stevens said.

"Why will we celebrate his birthday?" Rosita asked.

"To honor him. We want to remember him and his work."

Mrs. Stevens showed us a picture of Martin Luther King, Jr.

"What is a civil-rights leader?" John asked.

"In our country, it's someone who helps make sure all Americans are treated fairly," said Mrs. Stevens. "In the 1950s, black people were not treated the same as white people.

"Let's find some pictures and make a poster. It will help us know what civil rights are."

Mrs. Stevens helped us. We looked for pictures in magazines and newspapers. We made a poster. We put it on the wall.

At recess, Mrs. Stevens put blue circles on some of us. She put yellow circles on others.

"Only those who have yellow circles may play today," she said. "If you have on a blue circle, you must just stand and watch."

Nobody liked that very much. We were glad when recess was over.

After recess, Mrs. Stevens told us about segregation. That's what she called what we did at recess. She asked, "How did it make you feel?" We told her we didn't like it.

"In many places in the 1950s, black children and white children could not play, eat, or go to school together.

"They couldn't even drink from the same water fountain. They were almost always put into two groups —one white, one black. That's what segregation is.

"Martin Luther King, Jr. thought
segregation was wrong. He wanted
to change it without violence. He
thought people should get along without fighting.

"His followers did not push or shove, shoot people or start fights. Instead, they marched in parades. They had "sit-ins," where they sat down and wouldn't move. Or sometimes they just stood and sang."

Mrs. Stevens taught us a song that
Martin Luther King, Jr. and his friends
sang when they had a march or
"sit-in."

We stood in a circle. And we held
hands. That's the way Martin Luther
King, Jr. and his friends sang the song,
''We Shall Overcome.''

During story time one day, Mrs.
Stevens told us about Rosa Parks. Mrs.
Parks would not give up her seat on a
bus to a white person. That made
some people on the bus angry. They
called the police. And the police
took Rosa Parks to jail.

Some of the people in Rosa's town got together to see what they could do. They wanted to help Rosa. They chose Dr. King to speak for them.

"Black people should stop riding the buses in Montgomery, Alabama, until they can sit where they please," Dr. King said.

That's why today, when you get on a bus, you can sit wherever you want.

We wanted to act this out. Mrs. Stevens said we could.

We lined up the chairs and made a bus. We put the blue and yellow circles on again. Mrs. Stevens was the driver.

"Blue circles must sit in the back," she said. "Only children with yellow circles may sit up front."

Then the children with blue circles
got off the bus. They joined hands.
They sang, "We Shall Overcome."

When they got back on the bus,
everybody sat where he wanted.

One day Sarah asked, "Where did Martin Luther King, Jr. live?"

Mrs. Stevens read us some library books about Dr. King. They helped answer our questions.

"I liked those books," said Billy.

"You can make your own books about Dr. King," said Mrs. Stevens. "We will put them in our birthday display."

I made my book like this.

The next day, Billy said, "I get lots of cards on my birthday."

"I give cards to my friends on their birthdays," Sarah said.

"Let's make birthday cards for Martin Luther King, Jr." said Mrs. Stevens.

"Where will we send them?" Rosita wanted to know. "Dr. King is dead."

"We can send them to the Martin
Luther King, Jr. Center in Atlanta. The
people there will be glad to know we
learned about Dr. King."

Mrs. Stevens wrote the address on a
big envelope. She put all our cards in
it.

"On my birthday, I had a party,"
said Bobby. "Let's have a birthday
party for Dr. King."

Everyone agreed. We made the
plans ourselves.

On the day of the party, we fixed up
our room. Mrs. Stevens cut out large
letters: "Happy Birthday, Dr. King."
We used clothespins to hang the letters on a long string.

John, Billy, and Rosita brought cookies from home. Mrs. Stevens brought punch.

"Since Martin Luther King, Jr. was from the South," she said, "we'll call our punch, 'Old Southern Frappé.'"

Mrs. Stevens put two bottles of cold ginger ale in a large bowl. She added a half-gallon of orange sherbet. After she mixed it up, she put the punch in plastic cups. And she put a cherry in each one. It was good.

"Dr. King had a dream that some-
day everybody would be free. All people would get along together. Let's
plant a freedom garden in his honor,"
Mrs. Stevens said.

She found a large box. First we put
in some gravel. Then we added some
dirt.

"Now we can plant our seeds," said
Sarah. We planted zinnias, marigolds
and petunias.

"When spring comes, we will move
the plants outside," said Mrs. Stevens.
"We will make a garden with plants of
all colors and sizes."

"Let's pretend we are flowers in the
freedom garden," said Tommy. "Let's
paint pictures of the kinds of flowers
we want to be and wear them."

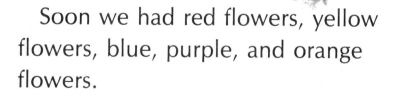

Soon we had red flowers, yellow
flowers, blue, purple, and orange
flowers.

We pretended to wave in the
breeze. And we sang, "We Shall
Overcome," one more time.

Martin Luther King, Jr. hoped our world would be like a big garden. People of different colors would be free to live and grow, side by side, in peace. That was his dream. It can be our dream too.